# The Journey Of Life

## Seeking the truth within

EMERALD K LEWIS

BALBOA.
PRESS
A DIVISION OF HAY HOUSE

Balboa Press books may be ordered through booksellers or by contacting:

Balboa Press
A Division of Hay House
1663 Liberty Drive
Bloomington, IN 47403
www.balboapress.com
1 (877) 407-4847

Because of the dynamic nature of the Internet, any web addresses or links contained in this book may have changed since publication and may no longer be valid. The views expressed in this work are solely those of the author and do not necessarily reflect the views of the publisher, and the publisher hereby disclaims any responsibility for them.

The author of this book does not dispense medical advice or prescribe the use of any technique as a form of treatment for physical, emotional, or medical problems without the advice of a physician, either directly or indirectly. The intent of the author is only to offer information of a general nature to help you in your quest for emotional and spiritual well-being. In the event you use any of the information in this book for yourself, which is your constitutional right, the author and the publisher assume no responsibility for your actions.

Any people depicted in stock imagery provided by Thinkstock are models, and such images are being used for illustrative purposes only.
Certain stock imagery © Thinkstock.

Printed in the United States of America.

ISBN: 978-1-4525-9050-9 (sc)
ISBN: 978-1-4525-9051-6 (hc)
ISBN: 978-1-4525-9049-3 (e)

Library of Congress Control Number: 2014900731

Balboa Press rev. date: 01/31/2014

# Question

People always ask questions about life. What is life? A blessing from the most high God, Love, Unity, Hope, Peace, Faith and much more... It goes on.... Therefore, it comes back to the same thing; Don't ever forget where you came from, In other words, finding you, your true self. Balance yourself, love yourself, take care of yourself and the list goes on...

On my journey of life, where I met and encountered many people, who have questions about life, and things that they do not understand. By love hope and faith there is no mountain that we cannot get over. No sea we cannot swim, but there is one father, many doors.

When one door closes, many will open. There is only one door to get there, prayer, love, joy, health, hope, faith, unity, peace and a will. There is only one way to get to the inside, by meditating, focusing, inner peace.

*First, you have to seek him, love him, as you are going to love yourself. Life is like a seed, if you plant or sow seeds, we expect it to grow. But, in what way?*

*Life is a cycle...*

*It depends on the way you look at it, in a positive or negative way. Life is all about loving, teaching and helping each other. We are the apple of his eye that we have chosen not to see. Therefore, someday we will find it. We are who we are to be. No one can change us, but We can change the way we think. We are all made to be leaders, when I say leaders, I mean of your own life. The father blessings fall upon us in many ways, it's like rain falling, some can feel the rain, and some just get wet.*

*Who can set us free? Only our mind, and ourselves. Do we love the life that we live? Not all of us. Do we live the life that we love? Not all of us. There are many things that can bring us far in life, like wealth and who you know. One of the most important things in life is integrity and the ability to affect those around you in a positive way.*

*Wisdom is better than silver and gold. We all have difficulties in life. We all make mistakes, but we move on with life. EG; quarrelling, quarrelling is a sign of opening doors, but what kind of doors. Doors to the light, or doors to the darkness. Love is the light that will never go out, everything done in darkness, must come to light. The ones who fight and run away, are the ones who will live to see another day.*

# Thoughts

Thoughts have a big part to play in the mind and the body. It can influence the function of the body. Do you think that circumstances shape itself, or the world? Do we shape our own destiny? Question: Where do you want your thought to lead you? Thoughts can lead you everywhere and anywhere. Thoughts are very powerful! Thoughts can lead you to good or bad. Let thoughts bring you to places you have never been before.

EG; a smile on your face, joy, happiness, and love in your heart. Everyone has authority over his or her own thoughts. You can exercise your thoughts in many different ways, but let it be in a positive way. Regular thoughts such as eating healthy, reading the Bible, taking a walk and time for yourself. Choices we all have to make for our self, for the rest of our life.

*God made all creations, man, woman, children, trees, fruits and the list goes on.... Do we all have faith? Yes! Do we use our faith? Some do, some do not. Faith, what is Faith? Is faith a question, faith is the answer to all questions. Faith can renew and transform you into a new mind of creation, with the light of the father. God works in our lives, in a very special way. He uses us in ways, that some do not understand. However, he uses us; and it always turns into a good way. Blessed are those who believe and have not seen. Blessed are those who have seen and still believe. With the father death, is not the end, it is a new beginning. Is there a beginning an end in life, yes there is, but in what way In the way we think, the things we do, it is the beginning of a new energy.*

*What is energy? We all have energy negative and positive. EG; a battery, which has two poles north and south, negative and positive. Which have the power to move things, such as machines. Therefore, the list goes on... There is a difference in life and in the mind. That is just an example. Can we strive or soar. Is there something in life to live for?*

*Tupac- "If you cannot find something to live for, you best fined something to die for". In life there are going to be some things that is going to make it hard to smile. Whatever you may do, through all the rain and the pain. You have to smile for me now, remember that is inspirational. Negative words are powerful in this world today. We say what we like, but words are very powerful. Do we try to understand that the words that come out of our mouths can do a lot of damage? Can we take words back? No.*

*Eminem - "The truth is you don't know what is going to happen tomorrow. Life is a crazy ride, and nothing is guaranteed, but only by faith" Michael Jackson - If you enter into this world knowing that you are loved, and you leave this world knowing the same, then everything in between can be dealt with".*

*Knowledge is Power! In addition, some of these people have that knowledge Tupac, Bob Marley, Michael Jackson, Martin Luther King and many more... These people had that knowledge to bring messages through their music. Music is inspirational it brings hope; it is a good thing to be inspired.*

*The father said love one another, because we are one big family. Ask and you shall receive, knock and it shall be opened, seek and you shall find. Jesus repeatedly reminds us what we receive will be the result of what we believe. Even to think lustfully in the mind is it a sin? Leave it up to you to answer.*

*There are many believers out there that question their faith. Because they get caught up in everything the world has to offer. We should not be afraid of new things that happen in our lives. Courage, when we step out in faith and courage, that is when the enemy comes out, and we face more challenges in our life. God said he will never leave us or forsake us. Because he loves us unconditionally. We all have and had experienced in our life.*

# *(Example)*

*Thinking, Talking, and worrying about what you do not want can never bring you what you do want. John 3:16, God loves you: For God so love the world that he give his only begotten son, that who so ever believeth in him shall not perish but have everlasting life.*

*When we are up to nothing God is up to something. Do you know that Gods love us is greater than all human understanding by sending his only son to die for us, sacrifice? What does the word sacrifice mean? Love, Time, Patience and the list goes on. Paying a price for someone else mistake, but it comes back to time and love. Love your brother as you would love yourself. We all shed blood but we never shed blood that Jesus shed on the cross for us. One of the worst thing than death in life is betrayal. Human being can conceive death but cannot conceive Betrayal.*

*If we do not stand for something, then we can fall for anything, in most of our life. We think that we should be accepted by others first before we could be proven acceptable to ourselves. EG; asking and praying for sunshine, but going out with your umbrella.*

*Like I said earlier, the mind can bring you anywhere and everywhere. It's like having hope, with a question mark. Hoping for the best but secretly fearing for the worst.*

*What or who is a true friend to you? God because he is the one who will overlook your failures and restore your faith. Everyone want to be successful in life, that is good remember we are all people of values, words motivate us, words build us. Bless the one that curse you, encourage, inspire, love and teach them. What do we do in most situations when we feel helpless, stressed out, and down. EG; get mad, and the list goes on.*

*One of the greatest things is prayer. Prayer can make a mile in your smile, and every mile in a smile can bring you places you never been before. Smile when you can a smile can turn into laughter. It can make your day and someone else day too. Go as well with a smile. In life, we all go through some difficulties.*

*EG; with family, health, marriage and finances, and the list goes on. Life is a challenge there will be mountains valleys to move, but how by faith. Faith can move mountains, life has it's mixtures of good and bad. What do we do when we are in a situation that is not going our way complain etc...*

*Things may not go our way every day, or all the time. However, we have to understand complaining will not bring you anywhere but in the same circle. At some point in life, we all have to grow up, not only in the body, but also in the mind. Old things shall pass away and be born again such as the things we do and say.*

*Those who live by the sword shall die by the sword. That is and old saying. The seed we sow is the seed we are going to reap. Sow seed for happiness, good health, love, hope, peace, abundance, security, and blessings on our journey. Not seed such I am not good enough, I am too big, I do not love myself. It could go on and on. Seeds like that can hold you back from your blessings.*

*There will always be a good thing from a bad situation. Life is what you make of it! When we think good and positive things, we create more good things to come our way. Appreciate and be positive and it will open doors to good things. Can your past define your future? Each moment counts every moment is a new beginning of your future.*

*Do we have control over our time? Time is important if you spend your time doing something important. You could make a difference in your life; time is everything. We could have the time for everything, but our self. Will you invite a thief in to your home? If you do then you will get the result. Just like your thoughts. Dwelling on things that could develop a thief in our mind, whatever you give your attention too. In that way you will experience it, you could invite a thief into your home and he or she will take everything.*

*Why not dwell on something positive EG; strengthen your mind, asking for a blessing. Love the one who created you, Love the ones who love you, Love the ones who hate you and love one another. Things like that could bring and attack even more blessing, and more love. Can a blind man lead? Yes sure why not. It is not what is on the outside, But what is on the inside that count. That is faith.*

*EG; going to church, what is a church. Some people think it is a building; we are the church in Christ. People that come together to talk about our father the most high, you are the church. Matthew 18-20 For where two or three gathered as my follower I am there among them. The word church take Out the letters u and r in the word church. Then tell me what is left their only Ch.___ Ch. Fill in the blank.*

*This is a prayer to the lord. Dear God thank you for everything, bless your name. I pray to you my lord for your blessing, your love, your strength, your health, your peace, your joy, your unity and every blessing you have to give to me, so I could share it with others. I pray to you my lord my God with love and joy in my heart. Knowing everything is possible with you. I love you, and I believe in you with love hope and faith.*

*I pray and thank you for your love and the breath of life. Your way is the way, the truth and the light. You are the fruit of my life; you are the blood in my veins and the love in my Heart. Thank you; continue to guide me on my journey in the name of Jesus Christ to do what is right, as you say lord. If you have ear hear me, if you have eye see me, in the name of Jesus amen.*

*Sometimes when things are not going, the way we want it to go, or hear the things we would like to hear. We put a question mark on it; sometimes we will hear and see things that we do not understand. Rather than questioning it, why not consider what God is trying to Say through that message.*

# Dreams

*Are dreams true? Do you think people have thoughts in their dreams are doubts. Dreams are private. Turn on the light and start being a leader, One day I think it was a Saturday afternoon; I went to the store to buy Some things, on my way to the store I ran in to an old friend of mine. He ask me, how are you doing and I reply I am doing well. However, he said he would like to open his own little business. He said he has no money. I ask him how are you, going to open up a little business if you do not have any money.*

*He said he had the money but he has spent it. I ask him how much money he had, to open his own business. He said it's been awhile. I said do not give up if that is what you want, by faith anything and everything is possible. Faith, He replied I have faith, yes, I reply everyone have faith do they use it.*

*There is an old saying if you want it that bad, you will get it, remember. There will be mountains to climb and mountains to move but life goes on. When we sow thoughts in to our subconscious mind, when you believe what you sow is what you are going to reap.*

*Redirecting our thinking from negative to a positive, going through a process of meditation, establishing mental pattern of drive, order positive energy into your subconscious mind. We punish our self, by the way we think. Two people could look at the same thing and see something different.*

*Sometimes in life all human beings are looking for answers for so many questions, the answers for so many question lives inside of us. Peace I leave you with, my love, my joy, and your blessing thank you father thank you.*

*We all have to understand life is a beautiful blessing. Some point in time in our busy life. We all have to take that time out not for ourselves, But for God and say thank you lord thank you. You can say I love you lord thank you for this day for the breath of life, and your love. Thank you heavenly father. We are all bought and pay for, with the blood of our lord, through our father.*

*God is love, God is good, God is great he is in my heart, every heart and he is in the right place. By faith everything is possible, what is impossible for man is possible for God. The grass is always green on the other side, seek and you will find. When you think he is not by your side think again he never left he's been with you from day one.*

*There is no other love like his love, on my journey of life I have seen and experience so many blessing and love. So many suffering but in order to get there we all have to suffer. When I say suffer the things that is going to break us, is the thing that is going to make us stronger.*

*Declare it by faith; Faith can move mountains we were born with faith and grow with faith. On my journey of life, I learn and teach the words of the father and the way to eternal life with love. Where the well stand I could only lead you, but you are the one to drink from it.*

*Judgment, what is the word judgment mean. Judgment is a thought in the mind that we all create by our self. Every thought that we have is a form of judgment negative or positive. Judgment is like a perception in the mind, we prescript our own thought and the influence of others in our life, Have a part to play with it too.*

*How do we forgive other? By forgiving our self-first and asking for forgiveness. The bible says forgive those who trespass against us. Whenever, you hear the word an eye for an eye, a tooth for a tooth. It does not mean if your brother hurt you, you should hurt him back. Why sell yourself short. It mean you should love him teach him and show him the way God works. If God is for us who could be against us.*

*Say you like someone and something that much, Example; you have a car, it could be your first car, and a car you love. You will take care of that car; you will take it for regular check-up to make show everything is in good working condition. That will make you feel good and safe that your car is in good working condition. It's like taking care of each other the way God takes care of us.*

*Blessed the ones that curse you, when are you coming back? Can you tell me? I know you are already here; your love got me going crazy, insane, Lord my God, in your blessed way. My heart reaches out repeatedly to you my Lord. Life is not hard, but challenging day by day I pray heavenly father.*

*Guide us into your light. You are the way, I will follow because you are the way your love is everlasting. Your love is peace and joy. I can feel you everywhere because you are the leader Lord, and I am your follower, your child, your gift, your creation and your blessing Lord. You created me in your own image. Thank you Lord. I am so grateful for everything and every chance that you have given me, to sing and praise your name, and to love one another.*

*When we are in our comfort zone, comfort zone, when I say this I mean for example in a relationship, with friends family and so on. When things are going good in our life, God will test us, he will take us out of our comfort zone. He will test our faith to see how strong we are, or what we are going to do.*

*God loves us he cares for us. We all have been test in our lives from the father. Sometimes in life the things that are going to break us, is the things that are going to make us stronger. God will use us in ways we do not understand. We have to trust in him, he wants to grow us by faith. By faith, everything is possible.*

*Life is in the power of the tongue, the message we give out. Some people say words are wind, but when the wind is blowing, you can see the trees moving, and when the wind is blowing, you could feel the cool breeze. However, can you see the wind blowing? No, but you can feel it...yes. How do you know when the wind is coming? By feeling its energy.*

*Do you know you are perfect in your own way, in his own way? We were all seeds before we became a tree, not only a tree to bear fruits, but a tree to stay strong. Remember a tree without strong roots will not be able to stand, everything comes from the root, and the root is the creator.*

*Do you remember the story about the wise and the foolish man? The wise man built his house upon the rock, the foolish man built his house on the sand. When his house had caved in and was destroyed and the wise man house still stands. There are so many keys for so many locks, but the key to the seed is by faith. It unlocks all doors, doors of a new life, new creation.*

*I read a story about a little boy who went kite flying, his kite went up so high, but when the clouds was moving in the direction of the kite there was no sight of the kite. The kite was invisible at that time.*

*A young man came up to the little boy and asked him "what are you doing" the little boy replied, "I am flying my kite" The young man replied "But how come I cannot see it." The little boy said, "You cannot see it, but I can feel it, by the tug of the string."*

*You don't always have to see or hear things to believe, not all the time. When you know, you know. That is and old saying. Can you control your destiny; our destiny is where our father awaits his children, in the house of peace and love.*

*I know*

*I know the Father. I know the son. I know the Holy spirit three in one. Where and when he lead, I will follow. My heart is deep; it is not shallow. The mountain is high; but he is higher. The love in my heart makes me feel better. His blood in my vein, I cannot complain. All I can do is call out his name. I need you Lord; I love you Lord.*

*Thank you. Thank you my king. I know the Father. I know the son. I know the Holy spirit three in one. His words are the cross, pick it up and walk with him. His words are the peace that will set us free. He was taken away only to set we free. He will return and I will still know thee. He is the creator and he will always be. I knew when I could not see, or feel you Lord. I know you are there because you care. You are My rock, you are my health, you are my strength, and my everything. I continue to thank you Lord, Bless you, praise you, love you and I will teach your words of love. You are the best. I praise your name father in the name of your son Jesus. This is a poem to our lord, from believing to getting to know him.*

# Question

How many of us know that there is a father? The creator of all creation. How many of us know him and believe in him. I do, many do and you should too.

There will be a time when we all as people have to come together Someday, where and when, time will tell. We all as people have to make a choice to do what we are here to do in this world.

Is this world a selfish place? We as people we make up the world, help whom you can and love each other. You could and should remember this love is the way. Can you remember the days, and the moment of the life, you have lived?

Most of us as people who live in this world. We live our life today, but thinking about yesterday and what will happen tomorrow. Why use up our yesterday and tomorrow in our today lives.

*The bible said in Matthew 6-34 so don't worry about tomorrow, for tomorrow will bring its own worries. Today trouble is enough for today. Every day is a new and blessed day. Everything God created animals, plants, human beings and so on. We are all bless by the hands of the almighty father.*

*Can we make all the mistakes in this world? No But we can learn from other people mistakes. This is just my opinion on that. Some people will look at other people mistakes and learn from it. Some will have to make their own mistakes to learn from them, that is part of life. We all make mistakes.*

*Sometime we see and hear things that we do not quite understand as people. I will say I have seen some things, that I did not understand myself. By faith, I will try to figure it out, and try to understand what it is, or what it can be. I will try to understand what my father is trying to teach me. Sometimes we will hear things; see things, read things, and so on. Not because we do not understand some of the things out there, into our everyday lives, it does not mean it is a contradiction.*

*Life is full of surprises, live your life. If I see the same thing happening repeatedly that means that, some thing or some things need to changed, in my life or the things around me.*

*My eyes have been open to many things lately. Things don't just happen, they happen for a reason. Words can be wind to me and at the same time, words can be inspirational to me. Not everything you hear in the world today you will take in. The world is changing very fast and so are people. You do not know who to trust, trust God. It comes back as everyone is for himself and herself.*

*We have seen this happen many times. What do we do, get emotional and get sucked right back in and then give them a chance again. God is love; do most of us do what we say? No. God does what he said. I know what my life is... a blessing, why try to figure out what other people life is about. I know where I want to be. Where I want to go and where I am going. Who feels it knows it.*

*This is an old saying, "Help the weak if you are strong" and if you are up look down from above. But when you do don't look for anything from it because it comes naturally, and it comes from God. It feels good it feels right.*

*Don't ever take kindness for weakness, every day I learn about people, people we love, People we call friends and people in our life. Know who you are and try not to let these things change you. Stay full of love no matter what may come in your way.*

*It is better to see the things that are happening around you now than later. It seems like everything you do for some people they never seem to give thanks. Not me to judge. God know when someone is grateful, because he see and know every one heart. Who feel it know it; if what I feel is wrong then I do not know whom I am. I will not question that. I am a part of my father the Creator. What I feel is love I know there is a creator and I love my creator very dearly. Because I know, he is always here for others and me.*

*On my journey of life, I have seen and heard so many things about people. When I am out there in nature. I see people as a creation enjoying their life. It is so beautiful to see what joy and love can bring. I see a creation no man can create on this earth and in this universe.*

*There are some things I will like to share with you, some of the things I have seen an encountered, with life and about life. I will not tell you are someone how to live his or her life. I will encourage them in a positive way, give them some hope and faith and something to remember, and to know. That will be you.*

*Believe in the creator ask him for the strength in your everyday life. Sometime in life, we have to slow down and take it easy come out of the fast lane take a break, take time out. We need time to think and to find our way back. Do not get too caught up in to this world and everything and get lost. Think about it for a moment meditate on it.*

# Question

*What you think life is, or what you think life is all about, your life.*

*There are so many different opinions on life, can life be what you want it to be. Do you ever think for a moment the life you have live and living has already being planned out for you.*

*The answers for so many questions for the people living in this world and universe. Do you ever think that everyone on this face of this earth and universe are responsible for someone, some thing or things? Is life a form of fining it's propose (yes or no) do you think you should live life as it comes. Fining who you are that's what count, your inner self an your propose. It's not all about what is out there, it's what on the inside.*

*The world is what it is. The people in this universe are all love by the one who created them, so love one another... love is the way the*

*truth and the light. The one who created love is the one you should love and have faith in and everything will fall in to place.*

*In life, you need a strong foundation. You need to ground yourself; life is not a joke, specially your life and my life. My life is not even my life. The one who give and created life is life. Don't be a branch in the life you have, be a root. A root with love, hope, faith, unity, peace, and everything pure. In this life you are living, in your life you are the root, a root that sow what it is going to reap.*

*He who is greater in me is greater than he who is in the world. We are all leader of our life. If you cannot lead your own Life and take care of you. Who will do it for you, the father of all? Life is what you make it. If you cannot help yourself, how can you help someone else, by the grace of God everything is possible. The joy of the lord is my strength, our strength stand for something in life so you will not have to fall for anything. We all have a choice and choices to make, make positive choices.*

*We all make mistakes so we can learn from them. One thing I know we are not hopeless, today we could be happy and the next day we could be sad practice bring prefect. I know everything around*

*us have a big part to play in our lives. Therefore having a solid foundation in life is very important, and having it with God. That is the best part trusts me.*

*Do you know the builder of your life? The one with the soiled foundation. The builder of all things seen an unseen? We all have a home here on earth, is it permanent. If you want to live a successful life, you have to cut off the bad fruit. Make sure you have a strong root and that root is God, no root cannot survive without the water of life. The source of comfort peace and love. I know God put people in our life for a reason, to help and the list goes on with love, unity, faith and togetherness.*

*Can you help who you fall in love with (yes or no) God did not fell in love with one, he fell in love with all the things he created, you and me, we are the most important being in the sight of the most high. When God gives you a gift or put someone or some things in our life. It is a special gift, because it comes from God, Guard it with your heart and use it to help others. Do not try to prove a point to the world and get lost. Whatever God has given you and bless you with do not let anyone, or anything take, it away from you. Whom God bless no one curse.*

*In life if you wait for someone or some things to change you will wait all the days of your life. God know every need, it is good to talk to him, he will show you the things you need to know. It is what it is, and it is what you make it. Do not forget that, the only one who could change you and me is the one who created everything. It starts with you first, if you want to change someone or some things around you. Why don't you start with yourself the way you think, the things you do, and the things you say.*

*The list could go on and on let it be in a positive way, I am just saying get to know you. A mirror is the best place to make that change, live your life with love and joy we were created to be happy and full of love. Do not forget where you came from, because where you came from is where you want to go. We have a choice and choices to make in life. The choice to find our meaning, and purpose and what we are here to do. Take your time watch your step and be patient, walk in faith, walk in love, walk with joy, walk in peace, and walk with the creator. Peace be with us all seek and you will see the things no man could show or do for you, unless God give him or her the power to do so.*

*The one that live in me is greater than the ones that live in the world. However, man could do the possible and God will do impossible trust in him the creator. He will guide and protect you from harm. Do not let any man or any one turn you away from the creator. Put on his shield of faith get to know your creator. We all have a choice or choices to make, as I said earlier to give or to take, to love or to hate, to lead or to follow, to live in joy or sorrow. The list could go on and on.*

*God is love he is everything you could ask for. He is the one to follow, his love destroys hate, and his love rejuvenates. All you have to do is get to know him in faith, with faith. My God, my creator is greater than all things seen an unseen. There is a reason for everything. There is a season for everything. Let God be your reason and your season let him be your strength, let him lead you, and let him guide you.*

*We will have to go through some tough time; Jesus said put your trust in God and in him. Secondly Jesus said in his words do not let your heart be trouble, my peace I give to you. God will take care of us. We can invest in every an anything. Do you know you can invest in the lord too take the time to say thank you lord. For forgiving* me, for I was bling but now I see, for I was lost without you but now I have been found. Do not let the world and the environment around you change you into someone you are not. Don't let the people around you change you in to everything they do and say. Let it be in a positive way.

Life has its mixture of good, bad, and ugly. Ask God the creator to show you the way because he is the only way. Can you stretch your hands were it cannot reach, so stop digging a hole for yourself. Likewise, some of us live by the day, some of us live by the minute and some live momentary on until they find the moment. Patience is the key to many doors; we look for success everywhere and anywhere.

If you look closely to the word success, you will see without you there would be no success so let come together in love and unity. Most people say it is the little things that count in life. I know that is true, remember you and me we were once little like a baby before we became what we are now today.

Do you know working together as one people make a difference? I could see the world as a place, a present place. I could see the fight to survive and some people are not making it easy or easier. It's like *a give and take thing. I know in life if you give you will receive. I know everything is in front of you and me. I know the creator give us what we need. He knows our needs, and our heart. I know if you ask you will receive.*

*The flesh is weak, try working on strengthen the spirit in you, the Christ in you. I see more takers and givers. I see the people with the little they have, give more than the ones that have more. God is love and love is God. Whoever lives in love lives in God and God in them. Take care, hope you have learn, some things from this message. Hope it have helped you in many ways. Thank you lord, may God continue to bless us all and guide us safe on our journey.*

# *A journey*

*First, I will love to thank God for life, love, joy, happiness, and peace.Thank you lord, for the gifts you have blessed me with. My journey started, when I was born into this world. A journey, as a sojourner to find who I am however my purpose and my meaning in this world.I live, and I experience life. Getting to know who I am. Living in the moment, living in the presence of nature.*

*Living day by day. As the sunrise, until the sun goes down. As the moonrise, until the moon goes down. Until a new day, begin again. Going with the wind of nature, the water of life. Listening to the sound of my heartbeat. Feeling the blood running through my veins, like a river running into the sea.*

*My heart guides me into the right place; wherever God lead, I will follow. My heart only beat love. My heart only beat joy. My heart only beat peace. My heart only beat what is pure and righteous. My heart is always at work, the love of God is always at work in me. Time will tell, as I live I see the beauty of nature unfold itself to me. I let go and let in the positive energy to flow through my body, with love, joy, happiness and peace from within.*

*A journey is not a journey until you go on a journey. Life is a journey. A journey is life, and a destination is death. Living life as it comes. God created everything in his own way. God bless everything and everyone with love and life. On my journey of life, God has and still blessing me with his love. Therefore, he is showing me the way to love. God has given everyone free will of choice and choices to live their own life.*

*On my journey of life, I have heard so many cry. I have seen so many suffering. A journey is to find, oneself, love oneself, and to help others along the way. A journey is to love, and to be love. One of the most important things in life is to be grateful, and to be you.*

*On my journey of life, I have seen so many people mold their selves into someone and something they are not. That is when you lose you.There is an old saying, if you cannot be you. Then who are you.*

*How can you be something you are not? Life is beautiful; life is a blessing from God.*

*On my journey of life, I have encountered many who live their life, as it is a destination. Life is not a race; life is a tour, to experience the beauty of life and nature. Do you think life is all about what you have, or gain in the world? No, it is about what you have in your heart. I have encountered many positive and negative beings. Most people are still living in the past. The past is gone, and the future is coming. The moment is now. Live in the moment.*

*What is our identity? Our identity is who we are in Christ, not what we have. On my journey of life, I have seen and heard about the things people dwell on. Things that will not help them. It is easier to blame others for our mistakes. Why be so quick to judge. I believe if we ask for a blessing and a healing, over our life, and on our journey. God will open the right doors for us.*

*Nothing is too big for God to fix. God is love, and love is God. God wants us to live with joy and love; God wants us to live to the fullest. God said he will never leave us or forsaken us. Everyone is on a journey, to fine the God within them. God lives with us always. No matter what, he will never leave us God lives inside of us. You may not see him, or feel him, but he is there. Listening to the little voice, to hear what it has to say.*

*On my journey of life, I walk in love, and stay in love with everything. A journey is not all about what you see. It is about what you do not see too. However, what you see now will all pass away. Furthermore, what you do not see will last forever. If you do not experience life, how will you know? What life is all about, and what is out there, your life.*

*Most people say seeing is believing, not everything you see can be real. A journey is part of what you do not know the unknown. What is the unknown? The unknown is faith, faith, what is faith? Faith is seeing and believing, what the eyes cannot not see. Faith is God speaking to our heart.*

*A journey is where our hearts lead us; it is not the other way around. Remember we all have a choice or choices, to do, feel or to be. Whatever our heart desire, let it be with love. Life is free with the love and grace of God. A journey we all have to take, to live, and to die, with love in oneself, togetherness and with one another in Christ.*

*We are living in a world that spins on an axis. An axis that goes around and around, just like life. There is an old saying, what you give is what you are going to get. What you give, you will not get back from the world, but only from God. God sees all hearts, and know what is in all hearts.*

*A journey to do the possible and God with do the impossible. Everything is possible with God. A journey of life and death. A journey of fear. A journey of faith. A journey of hope. A journey where love is stronger than hate. Every day is a new day, another day, give thanks and hope for the best. That life has to offer us on our every day journey.*

*Always hope for the best. Do your best, be your best. Be you, be grateful and connect with nature... our home. Fighting the good fight, fighting against the wind. Life is what it is; let life be what it has to be. No one has the power and the knowledge to tell us. What will be or not be what will happen or not. There is an old saying, judge not and you will not be judge. I think if you judge, or do not judge someone, someone will judge you. That is part of life; life goes on no matter what.*

*Do not take what I am saying in a negative way. Keep your head looking up into the sky, and keep you head above the water. Life is open to everything and close to noting. Therefore, we have a choice and choices. We listen to everything and we can be everything, but not ourselves. Most of us live, as if we need a permit for our lives.*

*God gave everything the breathe of life and love. From the day I was born, everything was given to me, from my mother, from my father, from my teachers, from my pastor and so on. They have given me, what was given to them. I am so grateful for all that was given to me, and the things I have learnt from them. Many people out there need love peace, joy, happiness, and our help.*

*There are some people that think that they have it all. They are the ones that brag, and never look down on the ones that need help. There is a saying if you are up look down from above and help the weak if you are strong. Seeing the people with the little that they have, seemed to be more grateful, happier and full of joy and love.*

*Being grateful for life and everything, you have. Life is a blessing, a blessing from God not from man. So stop praising man and start praising God. God opens doors, not man. God open doors no man can open are close.*

*A journey to fine the missing pieces of the puzzle. A journey to take. A journey we cannot escape. A journey that break us and make us at the same time. A journey once in a lifetime. Everyone have a chance, to live and to be happy. A journey of life comes with everything, the good, the bad and the ugly.*

*Facing life, how do we face life? We face life as it comes; all we have to do is be ourselves. Remember we are not alone. Love is the desire of our heart to live in love. We are living in a world where everything is divided into classes, High class, middle class and low class. Love is whole and cannot be divided.*

*On my journey of life, I have encountered many people who speak about how we should love someone. How to love our parent, our friends and the list goes on.*

*The greatest commandment is to love God with all your heart, all your soul and all your strength, secondly love one another as Jesus has loved you. We are all creative in our own beautiful way. We create things that make us feel good. We were all born with a gift from God, the creator. It is not what we have, that make us who we are today. It is who we are as human beings in Christ, and Christ in us.*

*Most people think that procession will make them rich, procession does not make you rich are make you who you are. They are just things we can invest into. Like cars houses and the list goes on and on. The things that were given to us from our past life and our thoughts have a big part to do with who we are today.*

*A journey to share. A journey to care. There will always be hope in what we do and say. The power of words builds us and gives us strength. So today let us declare a blessing over our life, and the lives of others. I have seen the fights and the struggles to make ends meet. As I said earlier the ones that have so much, they do not even know what to do with it.*

*A journey where everything sells, nothing is free. A journey where you will see many pretenders, people pretend to be something they are not. There are many wolves in sheep clothing. Just waiting for a chance to deceive us.*

*Everybody wants to be somebody. Be yourself that is all we can be. We have the choice to do the things we like, and the things that makes us happy. Let the joy of the lord be your strength, your light and your vindicator. When you feel joy, you see joy, and when you see joy, you see the strength of God in you.*

*We sow seeds every day. But, what kind of seeds. If you sow carrots, you will reap carrots. Do not expect to reap cabbage, expect what you sow. nobody want to plant, but everybody wants to reap. As I said earlier, everybody wants to be somebody. However, how much bodies want to be their own body.*

*We are on a journey to seek and to find. A journey where God speak to everyone, some listen and some do not listen. There is a word call intuition, everyone have it inside of them. Some say it is the little voice inside. Some will follow it, and some choose to go their own way. I have seen and encountered many people who say they need help. How can we help people, who do not want to help themselves?*

*On my journey of life, I have encountered and read about many who have lost their lives, and their love ones. The first thing I hear is what the family can get from their love ones death, whether it is a car, a house, money and land. We are living in a selfish world with selfish people. Most people talk about what they can get, rather than what they can give. Do not gain the world and lose your soul. I can speak base on what I have seen and experience on my journey.*

*There is a story about a shepherd who had to take care of a hundred sheep. One morning when the shepherd wakes up, he went to check up on his sheep. When he had noticed, one of his sheep was missing. The shepherd left his ninety-nine sheep and he went out looking for his one sheep that was missing.*

*Everyone wants answers for so many questions. However, how many of them are looking to find the answers for the question they are asking. As I said earlier on, seeking for sunshine. However, going outside with an umbrella. Hoping for the best, and secretly fearing for the worst.*

*I have encountered many who say they are my friends. A world full of wolves in sheep clothing. The bible said all the devil comes to do is to steal, kill and destroy. A journey where we need to keep our eyes on God.*

*There are many who will help us out there. Some will only help us because they only want something from us in return. Be careful, put God first in all that you do. The sun shines on the just and the unjust. There are many evil people out there. They are just waiting to harm us.*

*On my journey of life I have help a lot of people, and not one of them ever turn back to help me, or ask me if I need help. The only one who helps me is God. Jesus the son of the most high God, healed ten people with leprosy in a small village, and out of that ten people he had healed only one of them came back to thank him. God is the giver; he is the one that gives me the strength, to do thy will in helping others. They may take away everything from us. However, they cannot take away what God has given us, and that is our rights and the truth to share his love. When we take away from others, we are only taking away from ourselves. They may hurt the heart, but they could never hurt the soul.*

*On my journey of life, the only innocent beings I can say I have encountered are children. The lord words are, you can only enter into the kingdom of God, as a little child. You cannot enter the kingdom of God unless you become a child again. Luke18-17 Verily I say onto you, whosoever shall not receive the kingdom of God as a little child in no wise enter therein. God is always with us on our every day journey.*

*A journey we all have to walk through is the valley of the shadow of death. I am not alone and I will never be alone. You are not alone, and you will never be alone. It is never too late to make things right with God. Do it now while you can. God is love, God cares and loves us more than we can ever imagine. That is why he sent his only son to pay the price for our sins. God wants us to be happy, God wants us to come to him, and he will protect us.*

*He will show us the way, however Jesus is the way the truth and the life. God is our rock, my rock and your rock. God is our light, my light and your light. God is our salvation, my salvation and your salvation. God is all. Therefore, you should put your faith in him and in his son There is no other God like him.*

*This is a prayer to God. I would love if you will pray this prayer with me. Dear God, I come to you for your protection, your guidance, your love, your joy and your peace. Thank you lord, bless your holy name. I come to you as your child, and your creation. I ask you for the strength to be good and to do well. Cleanse me from the things that is unclean, in and around me.*

*Bless me with a clear vision and direction of my life. Therefore, I can live in love, peace, joy, happiness, good heath, success, harmony, prosperity and a faithful life. Heavenly father, in your house of love, joy, peace and togetherness I ask you to come in my life and guide me all the days of my life. Father God Shine your light in my pathway of life, so I may not stubble in the darkness of the world. Father God shield me and cover me with your unfailing love. Fill me with your Holy Spirit. Fill me with your faith. Lead me not into temptation.*

*The lord opens the right doors and closes the wrong doors. Bless the roof over my head; bless everyone and everything around me with your love and you grace. Protect me from all harm and danger, cleanse me and wash my heart, with the precious blood of your son Jesus. Lord, you know my heart; give me the strength to make the right choices.*

*Give me the strength to forgive. Give me the strength to release everything to you from my past life that is holding me back. Give me the strength to move forward. Thank you for creating me to be the person you call me to be. I receive your love and all the blessing you have given me.*

*I ask you lord my God, to break the power of any curse and evil words. That ever Being spoken over me, over my parents, my ancestors, my relatives, my sisters, my brothers, my spouse, my friends and my family, to be broken right now in the name of Jesus Christ our lord. Father God I accept your healing and your blessing in the name of Jesus Christ our lord.*

*I give you thanks and praise, thank you heavenly father. I am free from all curses, all evil, all darkness, and all unrighteousness in my life. I am full of your light and your Holy Spirit, thank you lord. I am walking with you lord in your light of love, hope, faith unity, and peace. All doors and all channels or now open to me to proper and to be successful in everything I put my mind, my heart and my hands too. I will succeed in your blessed name, with the faith; you have place within me thank you lord. Amen.*

*A battery needs to be charge, to do and move things; people need to be charge to live life. A world full of energy stealers, as I said earlier the evil one comes to steal, kill and destroy. A world where everyone in it wants and need something to keep them going. However, people of the world they come they take and they go. Why not help others instead of taking and leaving them drain. We are not machines we are human beings. Therefore, our energy comes from the source of life through prayer.*

*A journey where I have encountered many people, who love to compete against each other. Most people compete to see who can reach on the top first. I have seen many reach the top. If you like being on the top, keep this in mind, it takes a lot to stay on the top. Do your best, and do it with a clean heart, if you want to be on top. God will bless you for your good deeds. Make sure your motives are right. Everything that goes up comes down; remember a small axe can cut down big trees.*

*On my journey of life, I have seen people walk like caterpillars and slowly turn into beautiful butterflies. If we do not go through hard and tough time. Than we will not have anything to hope and strive for. God said seek him first and you will find him.*

*One of my co-workers came up to me and said. There are a lot of selfish people out there. All I could have done at the time was smile. He also said there are many blind people, who need to wake up. My reply was there are many people out there, that play they cannot see. Based on what he was saying to me, I reply. They are not blind they are good actors. Life is like a movie, everyone is an actor for his or her own movie.*

*When things are falling apart, God will put the pieces together. No matter what has happen and happening in your life now. When you stand with God, he will never let you fall. Therefore, you should stop talking about your problems, and start talking about your God. Likewise, put your faith to work, not your problem. Talk about the things that will make you happy, and full of joy.*

*We are all survives of our life. We have been through many lightning and many storms, and we are still here, by the grace of God. Whenever, we go through tough times in our life. We will always find a way to get through them. Where there is a will there is a way. By the grace of God, everything is possible.*

*We are not alone, on this life journey. Whenever, we go through hard times in life, we may not come back as the same person that left but stronger. God wants to strengthen us in our faith. God wants to let us know, that he cares and is here for us.*

*If we are not comfortable in our own skin, then how we would, be able to be comfortable with anything around us. Therefore, we need to learn how to be comfortable with ourselves first, and then we can adjust to anything that comes our way. Every day of our lives, is blessed and worth celebrating. If you do not celebrate life, then life will celebrate you.*

*On my journey of life, I had encountered with a little boy a couple of years ago. Who now became a man, and who dream of becoming a shepherd one day. He said when he was a little boy; he wanted to be a shepherd. A shepherd who can take care of his sheep. A shepherd who can discipline his sheep. A shepherd who can send out his sheep, so they can take care of the grasses. A shepherd who knows what his sheep needs.*

*Life has its bumps in the road, so we may not fall asleep on the wheel. Most people stumble in the daytime, than in the nighttime.*

*Most people walk in the light, as if they are walking in darkness. Most people walk and live in darkness, because they know they are the light in the dark. Life is beautiful, enjoy life because it is your to enjoy. Love life, live life, and be grateful.*

*On my journey of life, I have encountered many who talk about the weather, and nature. Saying it is too hot, it is too cold, and too much rain. People will go on and on, if you give them a chance, to talk out your ears, they will. Like I said be grateful for what you have now. Because what you have now, is what you can be grateful for. Nature is nature, let nature be what it has to be.*

*If you do not let things be what it have to be. Therefore, it will never be the way you want it. Look at the birds when they are flying, and see the beauty. Look at the way they soar with the wind, free. There are no chains around their feet. There are no chains around our feet, and we are not free.*

*Do you ever ask yourself that? Why are we not free, because we are all prisoners of ourselves. God will set us free, trust in God. God have this never ending and unfailing love for us. Therefore, love comes from God, love comes from one heart and generates into all hearts.*

*Most people I have encountered, say they are trying to find who they are. If you do not know where you come from, and where you are going. It may be challenging for you to live in the present moment. Therefore, people without the knowledge of their past history, origin and culture is like a tree without roots, Marcus Garvey wrote this.*

*The world has processes, and labels us as a thing. Separating the sheep from its shepherd, likewise a sheep knows its master voice when he calls. An apple does not fall far from its tree. A sheep does not stray far away from its shepherd.*

*Do not quit keep the faith, we are fighting just to be who we are, fighting for our rights. We are living in a world full of deceivers and lions. Just waiting for their prey, living in a world where we or fighting against each other and ourselves. Fighting for the things in the world, the things we cannot leave with when we die. There is an old saying naked you came and naked you will return.*

*How do we survive in this world? Do you think we survive by having a relationship with people? We survive with the relationship we have with God, and the faith we put in him.*

*A journey where we will encounter with many different religions, religion is what many are fighting to keep, Secondly trying to make a way for themself. Everything is a religion; my religion is my relationship with God. This life is all about having a relationship with God, and loving one another. However, God has no religion God has no favoritism.*

*God created the earth and made the universe completely not divided. How can we divide something that is whole? We divide it, by breaking it up into pieces. Why do you think the world was divided? I think the world was divided; therefore, we can reach out to our brothers and sisters in need for love and comfort. Moreover, it could be, to control us at the same time...*

*There can be many answers to that question, try to look at life in a positive way, Starting with you. When we divide, we take away. In addition, when we are divided, we are not completely anymore. When we are divided, therefore we can be control by the world and the people in it. Then we become no longer ourselves. If we are no longer ourselves, then we become nobody. Likewise united we stand divided we fall.*

*A journey of life, remember we are not alone. Furthermore, I will like to share some of the things I have heard of, on my journey. The words that come out of some of the people mouth I had encountered. My best is not to say, just be careful what you listen to, and the things you say to people. The power is in the tongue. The tongue has the power to say any things. The tongue can thank someone, him or her and curse them at the same time. That is how much power the tongue has. The tongue is a live wire.*

*There is an old saying, one tree from a forest can make a match, and one match, can be used to burn down an enter forest. I have seen the beauty of life from the eye of a needle. Everyone wants to control someone and something. Therefore, everyone wants to be in control. I see people tame all kinds of animals. e.g. dogs, tigers and many others animals.*

*On my journey of life, I can say I have encountered many who can tame everything around them, but not their tongue in their own* mouth. I have work with many people, who have no respect and show no respect. They say whatever they like, mouth open words jump out. As I said earlier, the tongue can do a lot of damage. The tongue is like a wild fire. Remember everyone have to give God, an account for every word that comes out of his or her mouth.

This is a story about a man who worked in a warehouse for 25 years and still working, on his 25 years anniversary he were given a DVD player, from his employer for all his hard work. A very nice and friendly man, who has done his job with no complain. The man I am talking about is a hardworking man.

I have encountered many, who talk about, how hard they have work and how they did not get anything in return. Whatever you may do for others, do not look or expect a thing in return. God will bless and reward you, humble yourself, or you will be humble. However your treasure with be not from the world, but from God.

Blesses are those who wait on the lord, they are the one who will find their way and peace within. We all have to work to earn our daily bread. Therefore, by the sweat of thy brow, man shall eat bread; however, man shall not live by bread alone, but by every words of

*God that comes from his or her mouth. God will provide for you, and his people, we always do.*

*There is an old saying only the fittest of the fittest shall survive. When walking along the seashore, you should be careful. Keeping thy eyes on the water and the things that is in it. The things that are hiding, we may not see them with the human eyes. Try not to fall into the water because, there may be piranha waiting. Life is all about survival, not in the flesh but in the spirit.*

*A journey where I have encountered many, who say they are my friend. What is a friend, and who is a friend? A friend is someone who will stand with you, and tell you the truth, No matter what may happen, in good and in bad time. A friend is someone who will love you for who you are. A friend is someone will comfort you, not run away from you, when things are not going well with you.*

*Therefore, you have an idea, who is a friend, People like that was never a friend to begin with. God is my only friend, a friend is someone will lay down his or her life for you and that is what Christ has done. I know he will never leave me or forsaken me. Just like we would never leave you are forsake you too*

*Life is like a crime scene, people come in put down their crime and leaves. I have work with many people, I have encountered with on my journey of life. Who loves to talk about how much money they have, and how much money they can save.*

*We all as people try to save some money for Rainy days. When I say Rainy days, I meant for hard and tough times, and for our children future. There are many who are working very hard, so they can buy food to put on their table, to feed their family.*

*However, there are many who are working very hard to gain the things in the world. The things they need so they can fit in with others. Are we working that hard to save our own soul? Do not gain the world and lose who you are. Your soul worth more than the things in the world, everything you see and have now, will fade away and the things you do not see will last forever.*

*Indeed the love of God will last forever. In addition, many have already given up his love for the world. Furthermore, if you are not from him you are from the world.*

*There are many powerful and evil people out there, who will give us what we need. They are like leeches waiting to suck us dry, so be careful whom you let in your cycle and your life. Everything has a price tag; nothing is free, except God love for us.*

*I have encountered many people. Who love to keep everything around them clean and spotless. Therefore, if everything around is so clean. What about the inside, Is the inside that clean as well? According to many I have encountered with, also said not everything you see on the outside is what it seen to be.*

*I know we are not perfect and we make mistakes. Therefore, you should not judge a book by its cover. The words that comes out from many people mouth, can give you an idea of whom you are associating with.*

*We are all program to tell others what to do, and how they should do it. Secondly, we try to change people into being, what they are not. If we can take the log in our eyes out first, then we can see clearly to help others take out the speck in their eyes.*

*I have seen and encountered many people, furthermore one out of that many, have showed me their hope and their faith. In saying, believe everything is possible with the love of God and you will see his glory. Therefore, the hope and faith, I have seen in that one out of that many can bring people together with love, hope, faith and unity. Therefore, it only takes one seed to grow into a tree.*

*A journey where I can say I have encountered, one spark can make a fire and one match can burn down an entire forest. Therefore, Christ was only one man and because he was one man, sent by God. The world and many was against him. They hated him because he was speaking the truth.*

*The lord words seek and you shall find. Therefore, you should seek the truth within and it will set you free, and stand up for your rights. Lastly, that is all you have, otherwise people will walk all over you.*

*There are many people, who will try to push us in front and use us as bait. As I said earlier, we are living in such a selfish world. Everyone wants more and more, the power and the fame. Therefore, most people will do almost anything to get what they want. They do not care how they get it, as long as they get it. The world we are living in is a selfish world.*

*Do you think Life has a limit? Yes. I think there are limits to some things. Where man can go, and cannot go. There are limits to how high man can go up into the sky, and how low man can go into the depth of the sea. We are living in a world full of fear. We limit ourselves by the way we think. The things we do and say, likewise, the person we choose to be.*

*On my journey of life, I have encountered many people that ask for my help. My reply, or, are you willing and able to let me help you help you. If not, do not waste my time. However many will ask me how much will it cost them or how much they have to pay me to help them, my reply is all you have to do is pay attention.*

*How can we take these people serious? I understand in life, there are many people that are in need of our help. Therefore, they are putting in the effort to get the help they need. I have encountered many who said they had to try, and fail before they can fail to try.*

*It is like planting and sowing seeds. When we sow seeds, we have to wait patiently for the harvest. I will say to the people I have encountered; patience is the key to happiness and much more. Most of the people I have encountered will say they have patient.*

*Life is like a standard car, you have to know how to drive it. Life is like a game, you have to know how to play it. Life is like a chain, we are seeking to find the missing link. We were all born as a baby; we were never born as a man and a woman. However, as we grow, we grow into becoming a man and a woman.*

*Most people live life like it is a destination. Life is a journey and we all as human beings; have to go on that journey. Therefore, take that journey. Otherwise, we may never know what our journey is, and where it may lead.*

*There are no short cuts to life; we have to face life, just as if we have to face death. A journey where we have to accept life and death, there are no escape to these things in our life. A journey of life is walking into the valley of the shadow of death, therefore the living walking among the dead.*

*As I walk through the valley of the shadow of death, I used to feel fear and afraid, but now I fear no one. My only fear is God. Psalm 56; 3- 4, When I am afraid, I put my trust in you. In God, whose word I praise, in God I trust; I shall not be afraid. What can flesh do to me.*

*In addition, I see fear as a word and a thought of illusion in the mind. That been created by the enemies of our lord. I know whom I am walking with and who is walking with me. As I walk through the valley of the shadow of death, I feel so much pain and emotion around me. I feel so much people trying to pull me in with their negative energy. God has given the light and life into everything he have created.*

*On my journey of life, I have seen who was a friend and who my friends was not, Likewise a friend in need or a friend in deed for a short time. However, many people out there will say they are your friend. They are cowards and user.*

*They are the ones who will abuse our kindness. Therefore, we call them people of the world, who come take and go. They are also call gold digger and thriving. My life is not like a real estate, where everyone come and see what they can take and leave. Therefore, everyone is a sale representative, secondly his or her motives is try to sell us something, and lastly try to make us buy something. On my journey of life, I have encountered many people. Who would live their lives; as it were a mortgage, they are paying for.*

*The father has blessed us all with his love by given his only son as a gift, to the world. Therefore, we can live our life in love, and by putting our faith in Chris by severing him and being a service to one another. In addition, Christ has redeemed us, from the sins of the world. Christ Jesus has paid the price for our sin with his blood, which was shed on the cross, for our freedom.*

*When I look into the mirror, all I see is the man in the mirror looking back, saying you are not alone. Furthermore, staying strong and keeping my faith in the father. God is with us always; in everything we do, he is there with us. Jesus said by having faith and believing in him everything is possible. He also said the heaven and the earth shall pass away; therefore, his words will never pass away. He said he would be with us even until the end of time.*

*A journey where we need to strengthen our faith in God, through his son Jesus, and to be encourage by his words. There is power in his words. God specks to us in his words. We need to break these chains of illusion, that were given and place in front of us. Therefore, seeking and living life in a spiritual form, likewise seeing life not from a physical point of view on life.*

*A journey where there are meaning for everything we do, and say. A reason for everything we encounter with in our daily life. A journey where we live and we die. On the other hand, are we living to live? Alternatively, are we dyeing to live?*

*There are trees with roots, and trees without roots some will live and some will die. The ones that live produce and the ones that dies, gets throw in the fire, or into the dump. On my journey of life, I have notice that life may take us in so many different directions. Likewise, who is the driver of your car? Who is in the driver seat? Furthermore, who is holding on to the wheel?*

*Therefore, we need to put on our armor of love, joy, hope, faith and have a positive attitude to face the world. We need to know how to pick and fight our battles in our everyday life. Sometimes life may knock us down, it depends on how long we chose to stay down.*

*Whenever you get knock down by others, make sure you fall on your knees, or on your back.*

*When you fall on your knees, you will be in the right position to pray, and when you fall on your back, you would be looking up into the heavens. Therefore, the light of the father will be shining down upon you, however giving you the strength to get right back up on your feet. Every day we go out to face life, and new challenges. Also not knowing what to expect, therefore hoping for the best. It's like walking in, and through a battlefield filled with mines.*

*On my journey, I have encountered and seen the ability to work together with other, toward a common vision for freedom, love and togetherness, with the ones who are standing and fighting for their rights. I see hope, faith, and a way in accomplishing the fuel to keep the fire going, and to see the common people attain the uncommon result. Like I said, stand for something so you would not fall for anything. God shines his light for everyone to see, a light that no one can put out. The light has taken away the darkness of the world, however in shining in our pathway of life in fining true love and happiness.*

*Many people are still seeking the truth; and seeking the redeemer of their life. God created all the nations to unity as one, and the selfish ones are trying to divide it. God has given us his words the bible, as a map and a guide to help us find our way through life with his help.*

*A journey where I have seen jealousy fall like rain drops and envy over flow destroying many lives. I have encountered a young man who was speaking about jealousy, he say there are little and big jealousy. Than he told me a story about one of his relative, he had work with. However, he was jealousy of him, because he had something his relative did not have. He also said his relative have even more than what he had.*

*My reply, jealousy is jealous; is there such thing as little and big jealousy? Does it matter who is jealous of you, and what you have. God is not jealous of us, People are. There will always have people who will be jealous of us. It does not matter what you do or what you have. Whom God bless no one curses. Furthermore, what is yours is yours; and no one can take it away for you.*

*In Corinthian 13; 4-7 Love is patient and is kind. Love is not jealous, boastful, proud, or rude. It does not demand its own way. It is not irritable, and it keeps no record of being wrong. It does not rejoice about injustice but rejoices whenever the truth wins out. Love never gives up never lose faith, is always hopeful, and endures through every circumstance. However, love is the greatest.*

*A journey to lead or to follow, everyone is a leader in their own way. On my journey of life, I have heard, the older heads say, show me your friends and I will tell you who you are. I have encountered and seen many Judas and eves on my journey of life. Therefore, we should be more aware, of the people that are hiding them sleeves in sheep clothing, also the ones that pretend to be something they are not.*

*This is a journey of life where God people need to keep their eyes on the price he have for us. I have encountered many weapons, that were form against me, but not one of them ever got the chance to prosper. Therefore, no weapon form against me will ever prosper.*

*Greater is he who lives in me is greater than the ones that live in the world.*

# A Prayer for strength and Guidance

*Lamb of God, who takes away the sins of the world have mercy on me. Thank you very much I love you. I feel your love flowing through my body, when you say you love me, and when my heart cries out to you, you hear me, and said come to me. I come to you o lord, my God for your strength and your protection, over my life.*

*You know my heart, and you know what my heart need. Thank you for your forgiveness, and your unfailing love. Thank you for listening to my heart. Thank you, for sending you son to save us from the world of evil people and the evil in it. Thank you for conquering death with your blood of love.*

*Thank you for sending your holy spirit to fill me with light, love, faith, hope, peace, wisdom and understand. Thank you for making me one of your sheep of your pastures. Thank you for guiding me on my journey of life, to experience and to see the things you have blessed me with.*

*Thank you for the grateful heart you have placed with in me, and your love, you have made it with. May your love shine through me, and the ones that need your love and your grace. Thank you for filling the empty hole, with your love, joy, faith, happiness and your peace. I give you thanks and praise, o lord with all my heart, all my soul, all my mind, all my strength and with my spirit of love with in. I love you now and forever. Give me the hope, the faith and the strength to never turn away from you, father God amen.*

*A journey where I have encountered and see many hypocrisy, popping up like popcorn. I have seen the light shining, and bringing out all the hypocrisy around me. The ones, that specks nice in my face and then try to harm me at the same time. Therefore, everything in the dark must come to the light, secondly everything behind closes doors will becomes known.*

*A journey of things I have encountered that been writing into the holy book, the bible. The lord always shows his people the things they need to see. As I said earlier, people are good actors; they play their part very well. However, what some of them do not remember, that all movies has and end, furthermore nothing lasts forever.*

*A journey where everyone acts, likewise many of us may and will encounter with the ones who do not like to take responsibilities and accountabilities for their own actions.*

*I have encountered many people who love to talk about love. The ones in their life and the ones who bring them joy and love. Likewise, many people will say they love someone for who they are, and secretly trying to change them to be who they want them to be.*

*How can that be, most people slowly change the people in their life to be what they want them to be. However, when you try to change someone in your life to be want you want him or her to be. Therefore, that person becomes something you wanted them to be.*

*Now that person becomes a mirror of the person that tries to change them. Secondly, that person will complain to the person they have change. Most people can adjust to sustain things, if you try to change someone, you would get the result and you may not like it. Therefore, you may even push them away.*

*Everyone acts like a slave master. Slavery were abolished a long time ago. Therefore, everyone can be a master of everything, but his or herself. I have been on a journey, where I have encountered many, who are still being controlled by others and the things in society.*

*Never lose your faith; God is on your side. Do not let or be control by the world, be control by God with faith, love, and his words. Call upon his name and you will never be the same, his name and his words have the power in them. God created everyone to be who he or she should be. No one should try to change someone to be something else. When God created everything, he made it to be good, to be the way it should be.*

*I have encountered many genies, magicians, astrologers, psychics, mediums and fortune-tellers. I have seen these so call people change the things around them, Make belief, with the illusion before our eyes. These people act as if they are God. Do not believe them they will deceive you. If you need answers, seek God first. No one knows what your future is going to be like.*

*I have encountered many doctors, who tell their patients you have this and you have that, and there is no cure. I can say I am not a doctor; However a believer in faith. Knowing that all things are possible with God, Christ is the doctor and the healer for all things seen and unseen.*

*Do not take what I am saying in a negative way. I am not saying you should not go to the doctor. What I am saying, is do not give the power to the things you hear or see in the physical body. Believe you are healed and you will be healed by having faith. Thought the grace of God, all I can do is encourage the ones in need of help.*

*This is a story about a woman who loves to go out and pray for people in the hospital. The woman I am talking about have a son who loves to rent cars. He was in and accident and he almost died. He was hurt very badly; he was in a coma for several weeks.*

*Finally, he came out of the coma.*

*He had several broken bones, but now he is doing well. I knew the young man from growing up and going to the same school. I have not seen him, since I had travel to a different country. We use to keep in contact; somehow, we have lost contact. One day unexpectedly, I got a phone call from him, asking if I could loan him some money to pay for his school tuition.*

*He said he would pay me back in one-week. He also gave me a date and a time. I said ok, therefore let me see what I can do to help you, again I said to him, I do not have the money with me. I call my mom (mother) and explain to her, and ask her if she can help my friend out with the money. I also ask her if she can go to my bank and get the money. My mom replied saying that she have some money in the house. Secondly, I had to call my friend back, to let him know that my mom was willing to help him out. The very same day my friend went to pick up the money. Before my mom, give my friend the money, my mom said to him, do not let me and you fall out for the money, I am about to lend you.*

*He said no, to make a long story short, the time came when my friend had to pay back the money, he has loaned. He was making all kinds of excuses, when my mom called him, he would not answer his phone. Therefore, my mom decided to call his mom, and the same thing was happening, up to this day they are not answering their phone. I did not get a call or the money back. When I call, no one will answer or return any of my calls.*

*All who love to lend money to people or so call friends, be careful God sees all hearts. Therefore, you should not take peoples kindness, for weakness. Remember we all have to give account for the things, we do, say and the thing we take away from others. Be true to yourselves, because when you are in need of help, and something in life, you may never get it, change your way of thinking and you will see the differences.*

*There is an old saying be careful what tree you back up on, Therefore, it may be the same tree you have to return to for help. Most people only make their way bad, not only for their selves, but for others also.*

*The people that take away from others only take away from their selves.*

*This is a story about a little boy who loves to play tricks on people. He always cries out for help, and when someone comes to help him. He would laugh and say I got you. One early Sunday morning the little boy when swimming shortly after he was shouting and screaming out for help. However, the little boy got a cramp in his hands. No one showed up or came to help him. Therefore, someone must have heard him and think he was playing a trick on him or her again. The little boy died, he has drowned.*

*I have encountered with some people, on my journey. However, love to complain about any and everything, never satisfy. I think people should be more grateful for what they have, and when someone is to help them out. In addition, most people help people out, because of the goodness in their heart. Likewise, putting them self in that person shoes. Therefore, it is empathy with love for that person. However, they do not have to show or do a thing for anyone; therefore, they do, it because they see their selves, in whom they help.*

*There is a reward for doing good, not from man but from God. All who do good for others keep up the good works. God will Continue to bless you, and give you the strength to do good. No good work is unseen in the eye of God. This is an old saying do good and good shall follow you.*

*There are many people in the world, which is hungry in need of help and striving from starvation. There is people who are dying from obesity, because they have too much food to eat, and they eat too much. There is people who are dying from hunger, because they do not have enough food to eat, and they do not have any food to eat. Life is beautiful with the love of God. Therefore, we should share with the one in need. However, we may have so much in storage, and storing up as treasure, our treasure is in our heart with the love of God.*

*Therefore, we should let the love and grace of God fill our heart with his love, in giving helping hands to those in need, expecting not a thing in return. In addition, let the motive be right in what we may do in helping each other.*

*I have also encountered many people, who would reach out to the ones in need of our help with love. There is a lot of deceiver out there; they are asking and seeking help to help others. When they know they are deceiving you. Most people want to get rich fast, so they do whatever it takes them to get there.*

*What is in the dark will become known in the light someday. One bad apple in a basket can spoil all the rest of the apples. Likewise, we should keep on praying to God for the strength to see and remove all the hiding weeds in our garden. As we continue to plant, water and fertilized the seeds of faith into our heart. As we grow into seeing the truth and everything around us more clearly. Ask God to continue, to shine his light into your pathway of life. Therefore, there would not be any room for weeds, to take root into your soil of love and life. Then you will see how beautiful your garden would flourish.*

*Life can be a bed of roses, and it can be a bed of wild flowers at the same time. The cycle of life and everything around us has been divided into classes, to separate us from the truth. Therefore, we go on this journey of life with faith and courage. Secondly, wherever, the construction is going on in our life. That is when we should start building our houses on solid ground, solid rock. In addition, putting our faith into action however using them as tool in getting the work done.*

*On my journey of life, I have seen and encountered many constructors than worker, many chiefs than Indians, many bosses than employees, many Gods than people and so much noise than quietness. However, there is too many hands in the pot, which cause confusion. Remember there is only one God, and two of everything he has made.*

# *Step by step*

*Thank you lord for the breath of life, for every step I take. Our father who are in heaven, give me this daily bread To do what you have written into my heart, fill me with your love, faith, strength, peace, joy, hope, endurance, and perseverance to be aware of your blessing. In my life and on my journey, as a sojourner, fill my heart with the things you want me to do. Speak to my spirit with your spirit father. Cleanse me from the things, I have adopted from the world, all the things that is not from you, lord within and around me.*

*Lord fill me with your holy spirit; give me the eyes of the Holy Spirit, To see and to know who is from you and who is not. Give me the ears of your holy spirit to hear your call. Give me the strength of your holy spirit so I may never lose my faith in you. Give me the faith to put you first in everything I have to do. Amen.*

_Emerald K Lewis_

One Saturday morning I went to the hospital to visit one of my friends. Who had a heart attack, when I first saw him; I saw that smile on his face and the beauty of love into his eyes. He was lying down on his bed when I saw him, he then jump up and then gave me a big huge, and ask me how I am doing. I reply, I am doing well, and I said hope you are doing well too, he said oh yea.

I complement him on how great he looks; he then said he feels great. To make a long story short, my friend is a very nice person. Thank God, for the people he has put in our lives. The faith my friend have showed me in being positive in faith and in God. However, it gave me the cold chills, knowing that faith is all.

What is impossible for man, is possible with God, all things is possible with God, through God and in God. When my friend said he is going to get well, he was being solid as a rock in God, and that said it all with love.

Jesus said in his words, what you believe in faith, is what you will receive. In Matthew, 13; 31-32 Jesus said that the mustard seed was smaller than all seeds, but when it was full-grown, it would be large enough for birds to nest in its branches. I knew in my heart that my *friend will be heal and recover soon, through the love and grace of God. Therefore, when God said it then he meant it. God cannot lie. God does not lie; he is a God of his words. I gave my friend a big huge and told him, he should get some rest. He thank me for coming and said see you soon.*

*On my way out of the hospital, when I was standing waiting for the elevator, the elevator came shortly after. When I were about to enter into the elevator, a nurse was coming out of the elevator. She was saying something to someone in the elevator. I then enter into the elevator, on my way down in the elevator.*

*There was a woman standing next to me, I said hi. The woman turns to me and said, most people she have encountered with, even the people close to her would say to her. You need to lose some weight, or you look like you have lost some weight. I then turn to her and reply, people will say whatever they have to say. Therefore, you should just be you and listen to you, love you for who you are. Furthermore, if you feel good about how you are. You are on the right road. What else matter? The woman left the elevator with a smile on her face. One smile can turn into laughter, and heal a broken spirit.*

*Let the joy of the lord be your strength.*

*In our daily life, we may encounter many people who would always have something to say to us and about us. However, it does not matter what we may do and look like. It is human nature to judge. How you look and what you do, remember it is not what others may think about you. Secondly, it is how and what you feel. About whom you are and whom you want to me.*

*This is the world we are living in today things has never change. Furthermore, all the thing that is happening now has been happening from the beginning of time. In addition, do or die, be acceptable by others, or they would make you and outcast. However, we seem to have more teachers than students now.*

*On my journey of life, I have encountered many people, who have spoken about their life experiences. How they felt about life and some of the things, which is not working out for them in life. However, in life most people think life is a one Way Street, likewise life is not a one-way street. Moreover, life could lead us in many different directions.*

*Therefore, in life we should try to be more open minded, however if we are not open to life, then we are close to it. We limit our thinking with a close mind. In addition, the way we think and see things. In life, most people would ask for something, and fear for the worst when they get it. Therefore, we will be asking for rain, however being afraid of getting wet. This list could go on and on, like a never-ending story.*

*Life is like a scale, therefore we need to learn how to find, balance in the things we do and say. Likewise, it may not be that easy at first, however it can be done; for e.g. babies, they were crawler before they started to walk. They fall down many of times before they have gotten their balance. In addition, they never stop until they got it right. To illustrate, more it is like going to the gym, before you start to work out, and get ready to lift the weights in the gym. First, you would have to do some stretches, and some worming up to getting your body ready.*

*Furthermore, before lifting the weights up, you would have to make sure the weights or the right weights, for you and it is the right size on each side. However, you do not want to build up one side of your body more than the other side. Secondly, you do not want to work out the right muscles more than the left muscles. Lastly, you would want it to be equal.*

*There is an old saying, when God cannot come he will send. God is everywhere he is always around us. However many of us do not see him, because we do not know him. We are the ones to give in to his blessing, and he would give us more.*

*On my journey, I have encountered a young man, who told me a story about his life. The things he has been through and encountered on his journey. A young man who was lost, betray by his own family, friend, and so on. The young man told me he was dying from cancer; he also said that he were taking chemo treatment for some time now; however, he is not taking it anymore.*

*Furthermore, the way the young man was explaining to with me. Indeed it seems like the young man has been through a lot and has experienced many trials in his life. In addition, the testimony he has shared with me about his life experience. However, has given me a sense of feeling, to be more grateful for life.*

*Moreover, the young man also said he have never given up hope. Therefore, he knew he was going to move forward and get well soon. Likewise, no matter what he was going through, and what may come his way. He knew who the healer is.*

*Remember, God is always on our side, he is always there with us.*

*Whenever, we may need him, in good, bad, happy and in sad times. All we have to do is call upon his name and put our faith in him, and he will be there to answer us.*

*Faith is what keeps us going, after all that have been said and done. The young man said he has found peace within, joy, happiness and faith in the things. That try to break him; however, it only made him a stronger person in faith and in God.*

*Always remember God is always on your side, he created us to be winner, and overcomers of our life .No one can take away anything from us, unless we give it to him or her.*

*The devil is always at work, and his follower is always at work too. Do not let the devil and his followers deceive you in there lies.*

*This is a story about fishermen, and how they catch their fishes. Whenever, the fishermen goes out into the oceans, the deep blue sea to fish. However, they are the ones who know the secret about catching fishes.*

*Furthermore, they would throw their hooks and lines into the water, as well with the beats on them, hoping to catch some fishes. When the fishes smell the beats, they know they have food to eat. The fish and fishes will take a bite at the beat, without knowing what is behind the beat. Then the fishes will be caught. However, the same trick the devil would try to play on us with his lies. I am giving you an example of awareness; how the devil works. Therefore, you may have an idea of what is behind the beat.*

*A journey to experience the good, the bad, the ugly, fear, love, and everything, that comes with life. The most important thing and feeling in life, is to find, you in Jesus and Jesus in your heart, in loving one another as he loves you. The joy of his love will bring us peace. No matter what anyone has said, or done. They cannot take away what God has place inside of us.*

*We are separated from the source of life. However, many will try to separate us from God, but they will fail. God loves us so much that he gave his only son to pay the price for our sin. We are now free from all sins through the precious blood of Jesus, by the grace of God the father. We can do anything. The love and faith Jesus has showed and put within us can move mountain. Father God I open the door to my heart to you so you can come in. The illusion of the things into the world could never stop me from loving you.*

*God have made us strong to be like bulldozers, to bulldoze anything that is in our pathway of life. Whenever, the enemies come out to attack us. They will not stop us. They may try to slow us down, but they will stumble and fall. Through God mighty armies, surround us with his love. Live your life, and live it with love, because love covers, and conquers all transgressions. Whenever, we are walking through the valley of the shadow of the death. God is with us.*

*Life would not fail us; it is the people around us, and in our life. However, everything around us is magnet. It pulls us everywhere. We are living in a world call a magnet field. Where, everything and everyone has some kind of connection. I have encountered many people. Who love to talk about love, and how much they love. What is love? Love is an action word, not just a saying word, it is a doing word also.*

*I have encountered many people who call their selves teachers of all kind. Some say they are teacher of love. Most people would speak of love; however, they do not know how to show love. As I said earlier, life is a journey. Life is an experience, of true love, to share with one another in the home we are living in.*

*Sometimes and most of the times we miss God blessing. We let people tell us how we should live our lives, furthermore who we should and should not love.*

*Two men went on a cruise ship, with a group of people. A storm came and the ship has sunk, and everyone had drowned, except the two men. However, the two men were great swimmers. They had to swim for two days. However, they made it to a piece of island they have sighted in the middle of nowhere. The two men were on that island for a long time.*

*The island became their home, because no one came to their rescue. The two men went to pray; one of the men prayed for a house, a boat, and food, the list goes on, his prays were answered. The other man prayed, and after he had prayed. He was just sitting there with a smile on his face. The man who got what he had prayed for. However, came up to other man and said, your prayer was not answered; therefore you need to get of my island.*

*However, as the man tried to put the other man of the island. A voice came out from nowhere, and said you have pray for a house, a boat, and food and you got it. Why, you did not share your blessing with your brother. However, your brother is the one who prayed for the things you have now. When you were praying for what I have given you, your brother were the one praying for your prayer to be answered.*

*One morning I went to the store to buy something just before I when to work. When I was in the store, I had encountered a woman with a young child in a stroller. I heard the woman said something to the young child. She said you are bad. When I heard what the woman had said to the young child.*

*I suddenly turn to the woman, and said to you should not have said such thing to the young child. The woman reply, She know that she are bad. I again said to the woman of the young child. Do you know when you say these things to the child. You are putting these thoughts into her head. She is a young child. The woman reply that is true and she left.*

*The good book the bible, quote and speak about the way you should grow up your child, and children. You should Speak to them with respect and teach them respect. Therefore, when they grow up they will not go astray and embarrass you. Parents do your part and your child will do their part too. In addition, parents you need to have some patience with your kids, just as God have patience with you.*

*I have encountered a young woman. Who said she had a hard child life, when she was growing up. She said she were treated badly. From the ones who supposed to take care of her. However, she said, she were called many different names, and the list goes on. She also quote how lonely she felt and all alone.*

*Furthermore, she illustrates more, that she had no one to turn too or talk too. As life goes on, she said, she knew God was with her all along. Now the tables have turned, from her being angry and full of resentment. She said to me, that she has forgiving her parents and the people who had contributed to the hard child life she has been through.*

*The bible quote you should honor your mother and your father. However, not everyone knows how to do that. The young woman I had encountered, said she have found the value of honoring her parents.*

*Therefore, parents think before you speak to your children, because what you sow in them is what they are going to reap. Likewise, guide and take care of your children. Indeed parents you are responsible for them, and you have a big part to play into their lives. However, they are God special gift. Lastly, we are all God special gifts, and he loves us all dearly.*

*On my journey of life, I have seen and encountered many people. I have seen the way they behave, the way they talk and treat their children. They are young and they will make mistakes, teach them. Try to have some patience with them. As parents and adults, whatever your child and children, hear you say and see you do. They will try to follow it too. In addition, please set some good example for you children to follow.*

*On my journey of life, I have seen many people show their love for one another in the eyes God people. There are many people, who are trying their best, as I said earlier. The spirit is willing, but the flesh is weak.*

*Pray to the lord, for the strength to overcome the things into the world. Pray for strength in the spirit, so you can be strong in the times of adversaries and testing. We are living in a world, where we are all programmed to the world system.*

*Many people live their life. Just the way they want to live it. Many people live their life based on how society and others tell them, how they should live their life. Life is part of finding happiness and peace within oneself. Never change who you are, because someone said you should. As I continue on my journey of life.*

*I have encountered, seen and heard so many things, where people beat themselves up mentality physically and emotionally. However, many people think that they are not good enough, because of what people say to them. If you live your life based on what people say, you will never be happy. You will never move forward. You will be taking two-steps forward and three backwards.*

*Decide today who you want to be, or who you want to adopted yourself to be. Try to make your own choices for you. Because you will know if it is right for you, are not.*

*There is anger in the word danger, Stay away from hate, turn your anger and hate into love. Reprogramming our physical thinking from a negative into positive from fear into faith and from hate into love. The love God have place within our heart, let it overflow with joy.*

*We are living in a world as human beings. Who have to be certified to be somebody. However, God has blessed me with my certificate, and that is to love.*

*In life, there is no limit. Do not let anyone tell you, you cannot do anything. Remember there is no limit to humankind, except the one we place on God.*

*In the beginning, God made and created everything, and it is good. Never let anyone tell you, that you are not good enough. If someone were to say something like that to you, just let it go with the wind. Therefore you keep what is your and you let go what is not you.*

*Anyone that tries to condemn what God have created are not from him. If you are not grateful for what you have now, you will never be grateful. A grateful heart appreciate life, it does not hate its own. Nevertheless, be quick to forgive and show love. If you take the time to look within, search for the inner child, you have lost along the way. The child you have left behind is trying to fine you.*

*Give way to God love to break down the walls of Jericho around you. When your enemy try to attack you, and try to eat you up. Just like the birds eats the ants, when they are alive. They will stumble and fall, as the ants eat birds when they are dead. We do not drown when; we fall into the red sea. We drown by how long we chose to stay captives into the water.*

*On my journey of life, I have encountered many who say they cannot do, and be whom they want to be. My motto to people, who think low and negative of themselves, and say they cannot. Remember can were made before cannot even existed. Only the truth can set us free.*

# A Thank you prayer

*Our father, thank you for the breath of life. Thank you for rescuing me an others. Thank you for your love, your grace, your joy, your faith, your peace and every other blessing you have place within me. Thank you for the seed you sow into my heart, to love, to shine and to share it with others.*

*Thank you for your shield of protection and faith. Thank you for calling me one of your children. Thank you, lord for the strength to say thank you. I love you, thank you for the strength to be me. Your love endures forever with the victories of your words and faith within my soul.*

*On journey of life l have encountered many including myself looking at life in an unseen way with love and faith. However living life from inside out, now seeing how caught up and asleep we were, in everything the world had to offer. We had not shown any respect to others and ourselves. In addition, we were living from the outside in. Whatever you may put on or in your body makes you look and be like it. There is a saying; you will never know what life is all about until you live it from inside out.*

*We are all on a journey every day, not only a journey to live for ourselves, also for others in Christ with Christ and through Christ in love. Likewise, finding true love and togetherness on our spiritual journey; however trying to survive the battle from the things of the world.*

*I have encountered many who say they have to do what they have to do to survive. E.g. If someone came up to you and say they are hungry. They have no food, no work and no income. What would do or say to them, will you turn them away as most people do.*

*Therefore, life could be a challenge and the things in our lives can be very challenging at the same time. Life is a test. Therefore, we should try to help others as much as we can.*

*However many of times people has approach and come up to us with all different kind of things. e.g. some may say they are hungry, they need money for the bus and so on.*

*One Friday night I was driving home. When I stop at a red light, a young man came up to me and ask if I can help him out with some money for the bus. He said he needed to catch the bus that was going to Hamilton. Hamilton is a place in Canada if you are wondering were Hamilton is.*

*However, I do not remember if I did or did not give him some money for the bus. I do not think I had a lot of money on me, Moreover, I always have some spare change on me and in the car; therefore, I had given to him. The young man then left.*

*To illustrate a little more, one Thursday night after work, I decided to go to the store to buy some fruits. On my way home, I have encountered the same young man I had encounter with a few Friday back. When I had stop at a red light, not the same light where I had encounter with him. It was a different light. The young man came up to the car, and then I roll down my window. However he was asking for money, furthermore he was telling me the same old story he has share with me the very first time I had spoken to him.*

*In deed a journey of surviving the battle not of flesh and blood but against the things in the unseen world. As I mention earlier on if someone came up to you and say they are hungry and they have no food and no income. What would you say or do, will you turn away from them as many people do. Alternatively, will you try to help or assist them in some way?*

*There is an old saying a hungry man is an angry man. I have seen and become more aware of the things around me. As people, get more and more vicious and desperate looking for a way out. A quick fix world we are living in.*

*Furthermore, not all situations are life and death. However, the endurance we exhibited should be the same as they were. We all struggle to keep our head above the water, weather it is mentally, physically, financially and spiritually. Therefore, do not give up; endurance can make the difference between sinking and swimming.*

# Thanking God for life.

*Heavenly father, Thank you for the breath of life. Thank you for the words to say thank you. Thank you for putting your words into my heart. I am so grateful, thank you for your love and you blessing. Thank you for all the things you have done and still doing in my life today. Thank you lord for everything, you have given to me.*

*Father God I ask you in the name of your son Jesus Christ, to watch over my love ones and me. I ask you o lord, my God for your protection over my life and my love one's life. Father God, cover my love ones and me with your blood from the lamb. Who have taken away the sins of the world. Heavenly father I ask you in the name of Jesus Christ to fill me with the Holy Spirit, wash my heart, my mind, my eyes and my feet on my pathway of life. Therefore, I may see and feel your love and peace in my spirit. Father God I am asking you for the strength to do what you have called me to do. Therefore, I can continue to walk in love, joy, unity and peace.*

*Father God cleanses me with a clear mind and with a clear direction of my life. Father God in the name of your son Jesus Christ I ask you for the strength to face the things. I may have fear, and the things that may come into my pathway of life, and the things that may test my faith. Lord Jesus shine your light in, on and around me everywhere I may go. Lord I pray and ask you to fill me with your strength of love, so I may never lose my faith in you father.*

*Father God I ask you to fill my heart and my spirit with your Holy Spirit so I can grow more and more in faith and in loving you. Heavenly Father, I ask you to seal my heart with your love, your hope, your faith, your peace, your joy, your happiness, your words of righteousness to overflow abundantly. Therefore, I can share it with your people. Heavenly father thank you for loving me blessing me and answering my prayer in the name of Jesus Christ I accept and receive you healing and your blessing amen. Here is a poem to illustrate what it is to believe.*

# *Believe*

*Believe in the one and only love. The created of all seen and unseen No man can save us, from this world. Only the son of the I am within. Believe not of this world, but in thy own heart. What is right, with the faith and love. That been placed within us the temple of the lord.*

*Believe in the glory and the grace of the lord. Our God and see his salvation. Feel his love flowing through your body. As the Holy Spirit take over our mind. Believe in your heart with faith. That Jesus is the one and only son of God. Who can mend the broken hearts and free the captives.*

*Believe that all chains are no longer around us. Believe we are free from all bondage and all depression. Believe with all your heart, life over death. Believe that no weapons form against us will ever prosper. Believe with all your heart, that you are bless and cannot be cursed.*

*Believe in your heart that we are not alone, and we will never be alone. Believe the ground we stand on, is where we came from, With the breath of life through the father of life. Believe everything is possible with faith and with God. Believe and you will see the glory of the lord shining through the clouds. Making away for his children's to walk in love, peace, unity and in the light of his unfailing love. Believe in your heart and with all your heart that Jesus is lord, the son of the highest God.*

*Believe in your heart that sickness could never ever live in our body.*

*Believe in your heart that the devil is a liar, and he has no power over us. Believe in your heart and pray that you may not fall into the traps; the devil and his follower have set for us. Believe in your heart that you can overcome every an anything that comes into your pathway of life, with the power of the name of Jesus Christ.*

*Believe; God is love, and love is God. Believe whoever lives in love, lives in God and God in them. Thank you to all. Take care I hope you have learn some things from the words in this message. Hope it have help you in many ways. Thank you lord, may God continue to bless us all and guide us safe on our journey of life.*